What othe

"I have worked with Derek in a number of businesses; he is able to combine the art of training and development with common sense based on years of experience and a real 'down to earth' approach. He works well with small groups and in full scale, Conference Presentations and his recent run of 'Street Savvy Master Classes were seen by many people as the best programmes they had been on in their careers, which for some was over 25 years".

Steve Pateman – CEO Managing Director, Commercial Banking AbbeySantander Banking Group

"Derek has helped me in a number of ways to sharpen my presentation skills.

I can call him and email him for advice and he helped me the day before I won the prestigious award in Perth".

Kerry Stevens – Young business woman of the year Joondalup - Perth Western Australia

With best Wishes

Derek

Sept 11

Introducing Derek Arden the only UK speaker invited to speak at the Australian speakers conference **Alan Stevens President of the Professional Speakers Association of UK said** *"Derek is the best negotiator I have ever met. This presentation will save you a fortune".*

"Derek presented the first Masterclass offered by the ifs School of Finance and is a regular contributor to the series six years later. This book is a must ....."

Brian Rawle IFS – Director - School of Finance

"Derek has been running workshops for our members for seven years. I would recommend him to anyone who needs an inspirational speaker, a presentation skills coach or a business consultant. He knows his stuff and people go away from his sessions enthused and enlightened".

Andy Walker, Communications and Public Affairs Director, Association for Consultancy and Engineering

"Derek has a unique ability through his presentations to inspire people to change. Over the past years I have seen him make a big difference to undergraduates on the Leadership Programme of the Windsor Fellowship".

Paul Toombs Associates - Advisers to the Windsor Fellowship Trust

"This book gives the secrets of how to present. It has helped me enormously in my presentations, particularly with my presentations in Seattle to Microsoft".

Richard Bassett – UK Branding Expert

"Derek is an inspirational speaker and coach. His new book is a must for those wanting to hone their presentation skills to a level of excellence".

Carly Read – CEO IconLive, Brighton West Sussex

"Derek's presentation skills are what I really admire. I have used him for conferences in Europe and Australia. A winner every time as he produces a Win: Win for my audiences. Read this book every time you need to speak".

Derek Ford – ACII - Insurance Broker and Conference Organiser, Perth Western Australia

"As a keynote presenter at the Sponsorship Development Conference at the Four Seasons Park Lane London he was the highlight amongst an array of top speaking talent. His advice is simple, practical but powerful. Derek's coaching has transformed my presentation skills".

Matthew Tumbridge – Chief Executive - Sponsorship Development Network

Presenting
Phenomenally

Turning presentations into fun

Derek Arden

1st edition

Tiptree House Publishing
PO Box 974, Guildford, Surrey United Kingdom
and ˙
12 St Georges Terrace, Perth, Western Australia

Presenting
Phenomenally

Derek Arden

First published in Great Britain by Tiptree House Publishing, a division of Derek Arden International Ltd, 2008

Copyright Derek Arden International Limited and Tiptree House Publishing

British Library Cataloguing in publishing data

A catalogue record of this book is available from the British Library

This book is dedicated

To Sally, Mark and Jenny

Thanks for all your help, support and putting up with me.

You are the stars.

Contents

About the author

Derek Arden is a professional presenter. He has spent 20 years negotiating, selling and training people. Without fantastic presenting skills no sale works as well as it should, often it doesn't work at all. So he learned the hard way.

As head of relationship and sales management for Barclays PLC Large Corporate Banking Group specialising in the retail and industrial sectors he has made many major presentations to clients worldwide.

Since setting up his management consultancy he has worked with clients in a number of countries. All his experience has left him phenomenally well equipped as an experienced practitioner, expert presenter and mentor. He has spoken to large audiences from places as diversified as Singapore to Stockholm, Melbourne to Monte Carlo and Vancouver to Vauxhall.

As a fellow of the Professional Speakers Association of the United Kingdom, he holds the highest qualification awarded by that professional body. In fact to date there are only 38 people in the United Kingdom that hold this prestigious award. He has spoken in 27 countries worldwide and has negotiated in 35. He has 8 publications to date together with many articles and audio programmes. His newsletter is read in many countries and he has a close following on his blog.

Derek has appeared on several television programmes including **"Demonstrating the use of body language"**, **"How to negotiate in a market"** and **"Spotting deceit and deception"**. As a life long learner he continues to attend conferences globally, learning and then sharing his skills

A consultant to many clients he has worked with CEO's, Members of Parliament and Boards of Directors to help them increase their profits, their confidence and their effectiveness.

The Chairman of Scott Wilson said after they floated on the UK stock market - "Each member of the Executive Board used Derek Arden as our presentation coach and adviser when we floated the company. Derek's help was invaluable – I would recommend him to anyone"

Derek is also a Fellow of the Chartered Institute of Bankers and a Fellow of the Chartered Institute of Management. A business practitioner of Neuro-Linguistic Programming and a member of the Institute of Directors.

He has researched the top presenters in the world including Tony Robbins, Tom Peters, Alan Weiss, Nido Quibein and many of the members of the various Speakers Associations around the world. This gives him a cutting edge in helping others with this critical subject.

Derek spends his time consulting, mentoring and running workshops in different parts of the world.

Foreword by
Sir Gerry Robinson

Businessman, TV presenter and author

Presentation skills are global. Wherever you go you have to present your ideas in a clear, concise and informative way. Your approach has to be interesting, fast and fun. If not, people get bored, switch off and don't listen to what you have to say.

In this book Derek Arden presents ideas on how to put your points across fast, with feeling and in a way that will make people take note. Use of this book will enhance your success and your results.

I have known and worked with Derek for over 15 years. He understands what makes people tick. I wish you well. By buying this guide, you have taken an important step towards your future success.

Acknowledgements

I have not attempted to cite in the text all the authorities and sources consulted in the preparation of this book. To do so would require more space than is available.

The list would contain professional speakers, libraries, management training departments of large companies, web sources and many individuals.

However, valuable information, considerable ideas and inspiration were contributed by Brian Rawle, Martin Kearns, Wendy Magill, Nido Quibein, Alan Weiss, Peter Hazell, Peter Roach, Hilary Wilson, Mike Elimer, Barry Cole, Paul Toombs, Matt Tumbridge, Tricky Bassett, Jim Ruffell, Jane Cranwell-Ward, Peter Thomson, W Mitchell and others, too many to name.

Thanks go to Brian Rawle, Martin Kearns and Kathryn Killner for their additional proof reading.

Graphic design and layout by Dayseven.
(www.dayseven.co.uk)

It has taken many hours of research, typing and proof reading. None of which could have been done without the help of Sally, my wife, partner and friend.

Disclaimer

This book is designed to provide information about the subject matter covered. It is sold with the understanding that the publisher and author are not engaged in rendering legal, accounting or other professional services. If legal or other expert assistance is required, the services of a competent professional should be sought.

It is not the purpose of this manual to reprint all the information that is otherwise available to presenters and other creative people but to complement, amplify and supplement other information. For more information see the many references in the Appendix.

Presentation skills are not a quick fix. Anyone who decides to make a presentation must expect to invest a lot of time and effort without any guarantee of success. Presentations do not write themselves and nor do they work without lots of energy, thought and preparation.

Every effort has been made to make this book as complete and accurate as possible. However, there maybe mistakes both typographical and in content.

Derek Arden provides education, training and coaching on Presentation and Communication skills in a number of different learning formats.

Workshops
Masterclasses / Bootcamps
Director's Seminars
Mastermind Groups
Coaching - Presentation Writing Skills
1:1 Sessions
Private Lessons
Presentation Skills
Negotiation Skills
Relationship Management
Influencing Skills

Website

www.derekarden.co.uk
www.derekarden.blogspot.com
email action@derekarden.co.uk

Other educational products by Derek Arden

Audio Products

Negotiating your Success – *Audio CD*

97 Negotiation Tips that the top negotiators don't want you to know

Street Savvy - *Influencing skills*

Teleclasses

Books and Pocket guides

---

117 Handy Haggling Hints
– *How to negotiate win win win deals*

The Secret language of success understanding Body Talk

Salary Negotiations - *The amazing secrets of how to negotiate your salary*

Street Savvy - *How to relearn Influencing, sales, negotiation and performance psychology in 1 day*
- Workbook and reference guide

Advanced Negotiation Skills
- *Workbook and Reference Guider*

50 Questions negotiators must
ask themselves

SECTION 1

Key points from the author

Your success in life depends on how you approach the millions of opportunities that surround you.

Having a positive attitude to life will mean that you are much more likely to notice opportunities than if you have a negative attitude.

Research described in Richard Wiseman's book the Luck Factor, showed that people who behaved in a positive manner noticed far more opportunities than negative people. The negative people just seemed to miss the opportunities as they passed by.

Throughout your lifetime you will interact with many people. The quality of your life depends on how you handle those situations.

The way in which you present your thoughts and ideas are very important. A good idea, a great business proposition or an exciting family day out, badly presented could fall on deaf ears.

On the other hand by presenting powerfully to our colleagues, business associates and family our ideas will have a much better chance of acceptance.

Good ideas need acceptance. Being able to present good ideas powerfully means we can help shape our own and others people's lives.

The ability to present and keep improving the way you present yourself, your products and your skills will make you even better than you are now.

Best wishes for all of your presenting

DEREK ARDEN

Guildford
Surrey
United Kingdom

How to use this book

This book is a reference book to be kept in your library and passed on to others who might need some help.

If you don't have a library at home yet, this book could be the first book in your library.

> *"The journey of a thousand miles starts with the first step"*

Chinese proverb

I was on a photography course in Alaska a few months ago. John, the professional photographer was teaching us that camera manuals should be opened at specific pages. Those pages should be absorbed one at a time, over several days.

It is difficult to read photography manuals, workbooks and even books on presenting from the front to the back.

If you read this book at normal reading speed from cover to cover it could take you up to two hours. This would not be the most effective way to absorb the valuable content in it.

Instead you could skim read the book once and highlight areas of particular interest to you for your next presentation.

Then dip in and out of it, reminding yourself of the things that you should be doing to make your next presentation even better.

It's your resource; *use it in the most effective way for you.*

Introduction

> *"What is the cost of not being a good presenter?"*

It has been said by many people that presenting can be one of the scariest things we do in our life.

It really doesn't have to make you anxious if you follow the tips, techniques and practical ideas in this book.

A famous piece of research by the New York Times found that standing up and making a presentation was scarier than anything including heights, spiders, snakes, dying etc. See details at back of book.

No presentation is the same – every presentation should be considered brand new.

If you can't present, you can't persuade, if you can't persuade you can't get things done.

> *To present is a present to the receiver.*
> *Make it interesting, informative*
> *and exciting.*

I heard that Bill Gates was once quoted as saying that there are more than 25m presentations around the world each day. Most of them are not of an acceptable standard.

In the 21st Century, because of instant communications around the world, audiences have much smaller attention spans than they used to have. It is therefore even more important to stimulate their interest using different styles and energy.

This is a real challenge for teachers and an issue that is being handled in different ways in schools, colleges and universities all around the world.

Confidence

> *"No one is born with confidence, confidence is acquired and developed"*
>
> *Dr David Schwartz*

David Schwartz the author of "The Magic of Thinking Big", which has sold four million copies worldwide, says that confidence is acquired and developed.

Confidence is learnt by study, practice and hard work. It is learnt by copying, modelling and learning from the best people in their field.

You can gain extra confidence in the short term by altering your body language and your neuro physiological state. Neuro physiological state is described as the mind body connection, how you feel inside.

However if you haven't done your research, homework and preparation, your presentation will be short lived and the only person you will be fooling will be yourself.

The problem with worry is that it is caused by fear. Fear can be cured by taking action. Procrastination fuels the fear. So convert worry time into action time on your preparation and practice to gain even more confidence.

TOP TIP - Never apologise for nervousness, never say this is the first time you have presented. All this does is bring the issue to the attention of the audience and devalue what you are doing.

The only time success comes before work is in the dictionary.

How large is your presentation world?

It is easy to forget the extent of the presentation universe. The places where you present and influence or you might present and influence in the future.

Here are some examples of the Presentation World, where you might present.

Business situations
Sales meetings
Training events
Negotiating deals
Motivation opportunities
Results gatherings
One to one meetings
Keynote presentations
Small group action planning
Analysts gatherings
Journalist interviews
Board meetings
Committee meetings
Facilitation events
Weddings
Friends gatherings
Clubs and associations

Make your own list

What is my presentation world?

1 ....

2 ....

3 ....

What will be my presentation world?

1 ....

2 ....

3 ....

Earnings and presentation skills

At the Henley Business School in the United Kingdom, where I was privileged to present negotiation skills for more than 12 years, they kept records, over a two year period, of the people who attended the Strategic Management Course.

The course was for delegates in senior management positions from all over the world, who had been chosen to attend by their company because of their high potential.

The records related to how their bosses and peers rated certain skills and how much they earned. The typical manager attending was responsible for an average 231 people.

The research showed that a small number of delegates earned more than 100% more than the average. These people had particular strengths in these areas.

> *Presentation skills*
> *Oral expression*
> *Appraisal of subordinates*
> *Self – management*
> *Negotiating skills*

Overview

> *"It's not about you;*
> *it's about your audience"*

Before you start, the key point to have in the front of your mind when writing, rehearsing and performing any presentation is that it is not about YOU. It is about your audience.

If you remember that, and deliver a presentation that is interesting, informative and relevant to your audience, it will automatically reflect very well on you.

Your objective should be to add value and improve the audience's knowledge, understanding and confidence.

If you go out to try and impress and make yourself look important you will almost certainly miss your objective.

So remember it should be a **Present** to **Present** to someone.

Keep asking yourself, "What are the benefits to the audience of this presentation?"

To have a great presentation, you and the audience need to stay present, in the present all the time. It is said that we get up to 90000 thoughts a day, so to hold an audience is a remarkable skill, and that should be your goal.

"Start with the end in mind"

Steven Covey, 7 habits of Highly effective people

Preparation

> *"Chance favours the prepared mind"*
>
> *Louis Pasteur*

The key to effective preparation is to start early. The sooner the better. Start thinking about your ideas the moment you know you are going to present.

The toughest part is getting started, so go for it, in a draft form early, and reward yourself for doing so.

The first steps to take are:

Buy a folder into which you can drop ideas, research and information.

Brainstorm all the key points you want to make and the things you need to research or look into. The list will change a great deal as you refine the presentation, so don't worry about it being right at this stage. Just get lots of ideas down.

Over the next few days and weeks, make a point of checking newspapers, magazines and journals for relevant current affairs. Presentations are always improved by using really topical content.

Go to the bookshop and look for books that can help you either with the key content, or your weaker spots, such as jokes (if you intend to include some). Remember humour is very personal. Test what works for you and what doesn't.

> *You are only as good as your last presentation.*

Rehearse. No matter how silly you might feel, if you want to make a really first class presentation you must rehearse in front of friends and family, colleagues or ideally a presentation coach. However make sure these are fully supportive people who understand the exciting challenge that you are facing.

You may feel embarrassed but you should also video/record yourself or perform in front of a mirror. You will be amazed at how this reveals things you didn't know you do. You will find you have nervous gestures or keywords that you repeat too much.

This will also enable you to realise if you have any "err's" and "ah's" that you can cut out. It is especially important to practise jokes and ensure they do work and that your timing will get the laugh! Be careful with jokes, make sure they are funny.

Stories, examples and anecdotes make presentations more interesting. You need to research the details of your story, so that you can really describe the circumstances. This is easy just use a search engine. Ensure that the story has a beginning, middle and end. The beginning needs to explain the main characters, location and circumstances. The middle makes the key point you want to illustrate and the end has some kind of pay-off. This is either a funny punch line or a summary of the moral to the story.

Some experts say that the preparation time to the delivery time is a factor of 20:1. I agree with the experts, if you are going to do all the work / research yourself, start early.

Practice makes perfect.

> *"The more I practice the luckier I get"*
>
> Gary Player, world champion golfer

Section 1
Tip Top Tips

1 *You are always presenting. Remember the extent of your presentation world.*

2 *A presentation is for the benefit of the receiver. Make sure it is interesting, informative and helpful.*

3 *Confidence comes from careful preparation, practice and thought.*

4 *Remember the 6 P's. Proper preparation prevents pretty poor performance.*

5 *You are only as good as your last presentation.*

My Notes

My Notes

SECTION 2

Golden rules

> *"In a world with overcapacity*
> *- speed is a basic survival instinct"*
>
> *Mindshift - Price Pritchett*

Here are the golden rules for presenting. If you remember these you will be well on the way to success.

You must always:

Set objectives for yourself. These might include the length of the presentation, the key point you want to make, the style or quality of delivery.

Have a clear outcome for the audience. What are they going to think, feel and understand when you are finished?

Set out in an introduction or agenda, what you are going to be covering in your presentation.

Test that the presentation makes clear the What, Where, Why, When, Who and How.

What I am going to cover?

Where I am going to do it?

When is it?

Who are the audience?

How I am going to do it?

Why I am doing it?

When the presentation is close, mind map the presentation to help you retain more of it in your memory. Mind mapping is a creative form of note taking, for more information read **"Use your head"** by Tony Buzan.

There is mind mapping software available at **www.mindjet.com**. However I prefer doing mind mapping on A4 sheets of plain paper turned landscape. Start with the theme of the talk in the middle of the page and then with sprigs from the middle put all the main points.

From the main point, put sub points that you wish to add, success stories, illustrations. Words should be in capital letters with small illustrative pictures where appropriate.

Confidentiality

- If you are going to use confidential information, make sure the client signs a confidentiality agreement before you present. However if you want to keep things "between these four walls" and are taking a risk on this then say -

"This is between these four walls, isn't it?" – at this point make sure they understand what you are saying from the body language

Or say

"This is subject to Chatham House Rules, isn't it?" - and check everyone is in agreement.

The world-famous Chatham House Rule may be invoked at meetings to encourage openness and the sharing of information.

The Chatham House Rule reads as follows:

"When a meeting, or part thereof, is held under the Chatham House Rule, participants are free to use the information received, but neither the identity nor the affiliation of the speaker(s), nor that of any other participant, may be revealed".

Source: www.chathamhouse.org.uk

Impression Management

> *"You never get a second chance to make a first impression"*
>
> Anon

Credibility is crucial. If you are standing up in a business environment, for example, planning to ask for a significant increase in budget and your shirt or blouse isn't pressed, your hair not quite combed or brushed and your shoes a little scuffed; you will have an uphill struggle to seem credible.

Of course, there is always the exception that proves the rule. But you will need to be really brilliant at what you do to overcome poor impression management.

When I am running a seminar people like to quote back to me Sir Richard Branson as the typical "scruffy" person. When I chatted to Sir Richard having met him at Singapore Airport after the world speakers' summit, he was smartly dressed, albeit casual, and looked the part of a very successful person.

There is a great deal of research into how long you have to make a first impression. Some people say a nano second, others 4 seconds. However there is a broad swell of opinion that says that after 30 seconds you have missed your chance. Most people, in this time, check your smile, eyes, and shoes. They also notice how you shake their hand, the watch you are wearing and anything else that might catch their eye.

A Managing Director of a large bank told me he nearly didn't employ a very clever 28 year old man, who had gone on to be a leading investment banker, because at the first interview he was wearing literally "Mickey Mouse" socks. What a risk that man ran without knowing it!!!

For more on this vital area, see my pocket guide *"Body Talk, The Secret Language of Success"* where body language is explained in much greater depth. This is available at **www.derekarden.co.uk**

So take the risk out of it all (you have enough to think about as it is):

✓ **Dress for success**. For a business presentation conservative business colours and styles such as grey or navy suits, white shirts or blouses and red - blue ties for men.

✓ **Have a hair cut**. Ensure you are looking well groomed.

✓ **Make up**. Even some men might wear make up if they are looking tired, after all stage presence is very much about the way you look. If you are appearing on TV or being filmed this can help you look your best. Many politicians will wear make up for television or public presentations. Some politicians wear make up as a matter of course.

One British newspaper reported that one particular Prime Minister spent more money on make up than his wife. They said it was at the taxpayers' expense. I have no idea how true that was, but the point is well made.

✓ **Think about your brand**. What is the overall message you want to put across? Does the way you dress reinforce the message of your presentation or does it conflict with it?

✓ **A white shirt or white blouse** is often advisable if you are likely to be in a hot or humid location, as this will not reveal perspiration as much as a blue or darker colour.

> *Casual dress can lead people to believe you have a casual attitude – dress for success*

On a speaking assignment in Perth Western Australia, I came across a company which has a Director of 1st Impressions. What a great idea. Who is your Director of 1st Impressions?

As a result I have now had some business cards printed - "Director of 1st Impressions" for my sales and consultancy clients. Send me a stamped addressed envelope to my business address at the back of this book, if you would like one.

"Who is your Director of 1st Impressions?"

Heather, a headhunter I was working with in London, told me of the nano-second test - she employs

1 - Look in the eyes for
> *Eye contact*
> *Energy*
> *Enthusiasm*

2 - Look at the mouth for
> *Genuine smile*
> *Hygiene with teeth*

3 – Check the handshake, is it:
> *Firm*
> *Palm to palm*
> *Genuine*

4 – Look at the shoes are they
> *Smart*
> *Clean*
> *Appropriate*

Self Management

> *If you can't sort yourself out*
> *- how can you sort others out*

When you stand up to present it is important to be in the right state, not in a right state!!!

Psychologists call it "state" but it is really short for neuro-physiological condition. We are really talking here of the right state of mind. It needs to be;-

> *Positive*
> *In control*
> *Focused*
> *Calm*
> *Present*
> *Well prepared and*
> *Thinking only about doing a fantastic job*
> *for the audience.*

You need to consider your physical and mental preparation. Every presentation is important and therefore it is important that you are at your best.

Get a good night's rest, have some breakfast and, if you are someone that takes exercise, consider doing some light training on the morning. Aerobic exercise is the best way to get rid of the stress hormone cortisol from your body.

If your nerves start to build, which is perfectly normal before an important presentation, practice breathing deeply to the bottom of your stomach (so rather than your chest going out, the bottom of your stomach goes out first). This crushes the diaphragm and helps you relax. Taking 4 breaths a minute calms you, whereas 16 breaths a minute, is hyper ventilating and stressful.

Think about the end of the presentation and imagine applause, positive feedback and smiling faces. Anchor the feeling when you feel the applause at its peak, by clenching your fist tight. Do this three times, clench your fist, at the peak of the strong emotion.

Every time you need a lift, clench your fist and imagine the same scene. Your energy will be lifted by this.

Personal Tip – Before a presentation I always get set up, test the equipment at least twice; have my mindmap fixed to the desk and my 5x3 cards in my pocket. This is my routine for confidence and to check that I am prepared.

Then I do the following

1 - I go outside into the fresh air and do deep breathing exercises

2 - I walk very briskly 100 yards almost like a soldier marching. Total confidence, bordering on over confidence that is what I am aiming to create with the physiological state being transferred to my mental state.

3 – I then go back inside, check that I am looking at my best in the Men's room. This is in case my hair has become a little untidy or my tie has become slightly undone.

> *"Look fantastic,*
> *feel fantastic and sound fantastic"*
>
> Tony Robbins

I heard a story once about a presenter who went to his doctor and got him to prescribe state changing drugs such as Valium or Prozac before a presentation.

I think this is extreme if someone has to go to these lengths and would never recommend it. However there are some herbal / natural remedies that can relax and give confidence.

I know someone who uses Bach Rescue Remedy which is made from extract of plants and is available in any chemist without prescription. Many people give it to their animals when they are upset in a thunderstorm.

NEVER – tell an audience that you are nervous. If you do, they will be looking for any signs of nerves, such as little finger rubs, twitches or anything that they wouldn't normally notice.

Building Self Confidence

Here are some gestures that can help **you feel more confident before a presentation** - (but only do these when no-one else is there, in case a member of the audience sees and gets the wrong impression)

These confidence gestures are –

- ✓ Steepling, putting the tips of your fingers together
- ✓ Crossing your arms
- ✓ Smiling to yourself in a mirror
- ✓ Looking up to the sky
- ✓ Walking with your hands behind your back (Prince Charles style)
- ✓ Walking 25% quicker than normal for a short period

These gestures will make you feel more confident in the very short term. However they will not make you look confident to an audience. Perform them alone and then, when you are ready; make sure you show confident open body language.

Routine for Self Confidence

If you are one of several and not the first presenter at a conference or an event, do as much of this as possible prior to the first person's presentation.

1 – Be thoroughly prepared.

2 – Check the set up of the room – make changes to your liking.

3 – Check all your kit is working – and the power leads are plugged into the electric sockets with the switches on.

4 – All handouts are positioned where you want them.

5 – Your notes are in a discreet position.

6 – Then 15 minutes before you are on - go outside and get some fresh air. Do a routine such as I have suggested earlier in this section.

Warning - Do not allow yourself to be intimidated by the host. Often they are nervous themselves and might transmit some of those nerves to you. Ignore any negative vibes you get and stick to your plan.

I read that Elvis Presley used to park his caravan 1000 metres from where he was performing. This meant that when the "five minutes Mr Presley" signal came, he had to walk confidently to the stage, getting that fantastic aerobic exercise that fills the lungs and secretes endorphins which make you feel great.

I once read that Denis Waitley, the best selling author and speaker, recommends shaking hands with as many of the participants before and after a presentation. It builds rapport, builds trust and builds confidence. I have now been doing this for a number of years and it works superbly.

When I am coaching presentation skills, on a one to one basis, I sometimes have difficulty persuading people to do the initial handshaking. One such person was a head teacher of a large school I was working with. She couldn't be persuaded to do this for a long time. However once she changed her natural aversion to do this "her mind set" she saw the results in the faster building of rapport with the audience who were usually parents.

Tip Top Tip - The mind to body connection is so strong and instantaneous that changing your body language will improve your mood and confidence and make you more likeable, positive and convincing.

Introductions

Introducers. Leave nothing to chance. If someone is introducing you, tell them what you would like them to say. Even better, write down exactly what you would like the introducer to say and provide it several days in advance. If they have any questions they have time to contact you.

I was fortunate to interview Mark Sanborn, the President of the American Professional Speakers Association, in New Orleans, Louisiana on behalf of the UK Speaker Magazine he told me -

> *"The details about you are much more effective coming from a third party. They have the status as the introducer and you can add in embellishments, which wouldn't be taken so seriously if you said them yourself".*

If you are introduced effectively the audience will be ready to listen and you are already winning. If introduced badly, you have an uphill struggle to get the audience's interest. Remember you are taking the audience's time; therefore you want them to listen to you.

Just in case a poor introduction happens, and they do, I can assure you, my strategy is this;

Thank the introducer and then say something like, "Just to add to that..." and then tell a good story or case study that explains why you are an expert or authority on this topic.

Before you start your presentation, say something warm and welcoming for example:

1. *"Welcome everyone, thank you very much for coming to this session"*

2. *"Thank you for joining us today.....*

3. *"Thank you very much for inviting me today"*

Sometimes I go into a short story / metaphor which leads to why the people should listen to what I have to say. It depends on the objectives of the presentation and the audience.

Enthusiasm and Energy

Start with enthusiasm, confidence and energy; these will be transmitted to the audience. Energy is contagious, both positive AND negative energy. They will think "this person has a message that he wants us to hear".

Other factors that can make a big difference include:

As you are being introduced -

Should you be at the back of the room?
Or standing by the introducer?
Or sitting by the introducer?
Or at the side?

To me it depends on the size of the audience and room.

The issue with standing by the introducer is that you are being watched by the audience as you are being introduced. If for some reason the introduction doesn't go well, the audience will be watching your body language to see how you are reacting. Secondly it takes away the element of surprise that is there as you walk from the back, and allows you to keep your physiology and your body gestures to yourself until the last minute.

As you will have gathered, I prefer entering from the back or the side of the room.

Timings

When writing your presentation, start at the end. What is the last thing you want to say to ensure you have got your message across?

Then prioritise the key points that you must make and note if they need to follow in any particular order.

Give each key topic a certain amount of time, depending on its complexity and priority.

This now makes writing the presentation easier as you can now write it in chunks (which is less intimidating or daunting). It also means that if at the last minute you are asked to reduce the presentation time you can drop your least important chunk and know how much time it will save you.

Ensure that you have a clock that you can see somewhere nearby. Many speakers take their watch off and put it in front of them before they start. I have a travel clock on the desk, pointing towards me

If possible it is also extremely useful to have someone who will let you know when there are 5 minutes left.

If you expect to overrun, and you have a very interested audience (remember you can tell this from the body language), then ask permission to overrun by a few minutes.

> *"Action is the number 1 tool for success"*
>
> *Napoleon Hill*

Opening

> *"The best spontaneous gags are the well rehearsed ones"*
>
> Bob Monkhouse, British comedian

Take your time, be cool.

Once you have completed your initial welcome or opening (mentioned earlier) you should cover points of business:

Hygiene factors for the audience to think about. This shows respect for the attendees:

✓ Ask for all mobiles to be turned off or to silent

✓ Explain any health and safety information

✓ Outline when any breaks will be

It is then absolutely vital that you tell your audience what you are going to tell them.

Depending on the objectives of the presentation, you may use some 'Yes Tag' questions at this stage to build audience support for your proposed outline. For example, you may say, "We are all here to learn, aren't we?" and "It can feel uncomfortable but, being interactive and taking part, really makes the day more enjoyable and useful for everyone, doesn't it?"

If it is a business pitch or business presentation, perhaps you might say:-

"We are here to present how we have the capability to do this piece of work for you.
It is our intention to show you how good we are and why you should ask us to work with you".

Section 2

Tip Top Tips

1   *Speed stuns. Under promise and over deliver. People are very impressed when others do things swiftly and competently.*

2   *You don't get a second chance to make a 1st impression. Practice.*

3   *Confidence comes with preparation. Prepare, prepare, prepare.*

4   *Enthusiasm, energy and attitude are contagious.*

5   *Get your timings right and expect the unexpected. Be prepared to change your timings.*

My Notes

My Notes

SECTION 3

Content

> *Make sure your content is interesting to the reader*

When writing your content, pull out your research file and look at what you have discovered so far. Select one of the key topics and look at how much time you have allotted to it in your plan. This might be a good time to mindmap your thoughts.

If you are using a PowerPoint presentation you should be aiming to talk about each slide for no more than 2 minutes (see separate section on PowerPoint).

However, remember PowerPoint is a visual aid and if the slide has made the point you want to make and you haven't got to the next slide make sure you blank the screen using the "B" key. Depressing this once blanks the screen and depressing it again brings the screen back. You can alternatively use the W key which whitens the screen. (See section on PowerPoint for more handy hints).

For each key topic, "Start with the end in mind". What is the key point you want to have made by the end of the section?

Ensure that you are going to hold the audience's attention by making the content interesting to them. You can do this by changing the style of delivery.

If you have just been explaining something, switch to a case study that requires audience participation or tell a story. If you have taken 5 minutes to explain a new process, take questions for two minutes.

When you have your content outlined, leave it for a day or two and allow your unconscious mind to work on it. It's amazing how the unconscious comes up with all sorts of ideas once you get going. Keep a pad with you because these ideas come to you when you least expect them and these NUGGETS need recording immediately.

Stages of Learning

Recent research shows that people have preferred learning methods.

The statistics are -

Reading	25% of people
Audio	25% of people
Video	10% of people
Attending a conference	40% of people

Additionally to this, when people can experience a role play, case study or even hands on learning it cements the learning into the unconscious mind faster. It gets them to unconscious competence more quickly (see below).

The four stages of learning are

1. Unconscious incompetence (we don't know what we don't know)
2. Conscious incompetence (we now know, what we don't know)
3. Conscious competence (we consciously do it)
4. Unconscious competence (we unconsciously do it)

When you are teaching or presenting, you need to be in conscious competence to get the points across to the audience.

Make sure you make use of as many of these types of media in your presentations as possible – handouts / workbooks / audio / video / DVD clips / visual examples etc to help your audience to unconscious competence as quickly as you can.

Visual aids

Use all multi-media as appropriate but make sure you know how to use the kit. DVD / Video clips and audio recordings can help you break up the presentation. If you have spent quite a long time explaining slides, refer to the handouts for the next point (assuming there is something that can be more easily explained that way).

I recently chaired a conference where one of the speakers had recorded the voicemail messages of some of the people in the audience. This was done to show how poor some of their greetings were. He didn't embarrass the clients with their names as these were deleted, but he made an amazingly powerful point.

One of the members of a mastermind group I belong to is a brilliant presenter. During one of her presentations she uses a metaphor which asks the audience to think, "Have they got their ladder up against the right wall". She takes to her presentation a ladder which she stands up against a wall – and moves it around, standing on the ladder when appropriate.

Think about what visual aids, you might take with you that will be an effective reminder for the audience. I sometimes take chocolate bars called TIME OUT, to remind delegates on a negotiation skills workshop to take a deliberate time out when negotiating a difficult deal.

A picture paints a thousand words.

When I am talking about how the brain functions, I explain the difference between the left brain and the right brain. This is mainly done via PowerPoint and some very good MRI pictures of the brain that you can see on **www.brainplace.com**.

However I also pass around an X ray of a brain scan that I obtained from a neuro surgeon at Oxford Infirmary, which clearly shows the left hemisphere and right hemisphere. The audience can look at this individually, hold it and touch it.

If you have a fascinating product, or want to explain something very visual, bring the product or a picture or video clip that can graphically illustrate it.

I was employed by a company that is subject to the Official Secrets Act to help them with their sales presentations. They make rugged laptops and printers for the defence, construction and geological industries. Anyone in fact that needs a laptop, which can sustain the inevitable battering of field work.

The first thing that struck me was that they didn't have a demonstration rugged laptop with them.

They now take their rugged laptops to presentations and drop them on the floor to demonstrate how strong they are.. The Sales Director tells me their sales rates improved dramatically with this visual and audio demonstration.

Whatever the visual aid, hold it as if it is an expensive piece of jewellery. If you treat it roughly, as if it is valueless, that is how it will come across to the audience. Hold it carefully, caress it, put it down as if it will break and leave it on show or pass it around.

Nido Quibein, President of Highpoint University in North Carolina (one of my mentors) has had some gold plated keys made which represent the door to the University.

He gives them to potential sponsors of the University and treats them as if they are made of real gold. The way he presents the gift makes the recipient feel they are very valuable. Their value is in their uniqueness and the way this brilliant communicator exploits it.

Demonstration

Sometimes a presentation can become a demonstration. This can be enormously powerful to increase the buy in of your client or prospect.
Always demonstrate if you can.

Prop Ideas

Apart from the ladder idea that I have mentioned earlier, here are some more thoughts:

I may take a bottle of Chateau Margaux to a presentation if I want to tell the story of my negotiations with Pernod Ricaud over the vineyard Margaux, which is in Bordeaux.

I take sunglasses if I want to demonstrate how you might feel uncomfortable with someone if you can't see their eyes.

I take a simple magic trick and show how it is done, when I want to show the power of preparation.

What can you take to your presentations?

Handouts

Handouts can be used in many different ways. I recommend first that you think about what is the purpose of the handout and how it fits into the objective of the presentation. If the handouts are notes to go with the presentation, consider whether you give them out at the beginning or at the end. If I am a delegate I do not like them given out at the end because I like to make my own notes on them as I go along.

Some people feel it is a bit patronising to think that the delegates won't pay attention to you, if they are reading the handouts. It all says a lot about you if your presentation isn't dynamic enough to hold their attention as you speak.

The options are –

1 Have them given out with the delegate pack.

2 Leave them on the chairs before the session.

3 Give them out personally, possibly with a small group and build rapport.

4 Give them out during the session – this can be used as a tactic to keep people alert.

5 Give them out at the end.

Make sure you know the location in the notes or workbooks of the key points to which you are going to refer. This enables you to direct people to them quickly.

Just like any props you use, treat handouts as if they are enormously valuable and that's how people will perceive them.

If you are going to give anything away that is personal, pick a time or a moment that gets you maximum impact.

Presentation books / Pitch books

I never recommend that a presentation of anything important should be made without the key people present. However, we know that sometimes a client may ask for your presentation in advance.

If this happens, make sure your presentation book or pitch book is fantastic. You might consider putting tabs in specific pages on which you want the client to focus.

"Pitch book" is jargon for a presentation where you are specifically "pitching" to a client for a piece of business. The book could contain league tables showing your company's position relative to the competition. They will also include testimonials from previous deals, reference stories from other deals, business rating if one exists. Further information should include points of contact within the business, specialists, manufacturers, relationship people etc.

Within a pitch book, you might include a great deal of information which would be a waste of time in a face to face presentation. Make sure your pitch books have the relevant pages tabbed for your client and you can move through them quickly . I have known people who have been unprepared, run out of time before they have got half way through the presentation.

Beauty parades

Beauty parades, as the name implies, describes those occasions when you are lined up with your competition and asked to present on the same subject or pitch for the same piece of business.

They are no different to any other competitive presentation but they can create extra pressure in the minds of the companies and the presenters.

Make sure you take the most appropriate people to the beauty parade to help you win the business. If the CEO needs to be there, persuade him to be there. If your boss should be there, swallow your pride, if that is getting in the way, and ask her to come. Make sure she is properly briefed and make sure you get her to sum up and ask for the business.

Team Presenting

Introducing the team is very important. Make sure that the client knows why each member of the team is there and how each person contributes to the presentation and the business.

Smooth introductions and handovers are very important. Use statements like -

"Thank you John for covering the area of production - now I am going to hand over to Kerry who is going to deal with how we propose to deal with the logistics of delivery"

Make sure that business cards are given out at the beginning and that you collect business cards from the clients. This helps with remembering names and gives you the opportunity to see the relevant status and position of the various people.

Line the business cards up in the position of the seating of the clients. This will enable you to use their names easily and without fear of making a mistake.

> *"In the corporate presentations world, most people and most businesses generally focus on becoming good enough or having adequate presentation skills. At this primary level, presenters don't fully appreciate the critical impact that presentation effectiveness can have on their success or that of their business"*
>
> Tony Jewry - Life is a series of presentations

Chief Presentations Officer

Jewry also recommends having a "Chief Presentations Officer", who monitors the quality of the presentations. I think this is a fantastic idea, as a company is only as good as the way it is perceived by the client.

PowerPoint

Is it a PowerPoint presentation? OR a presentation using PowerPoint?

PowerPoint is nothing more than a visual aid. A very powerful visual aid if used properly. However, it is often regarded as essential to a presentation as it shows that you have prepared and can make you look professional.

Remember that PowerPoint is an aid to help influence your audience's decision. Used badly it can become deadly boring for everyone. This is where the phrase "Death by PowerPoint" originates.

Here are some top tips for designing and using PowerPoint

- ✓ Use a personalised background
- ✓ Use a client's logo where possible
- ✓ Use bar charts and graphs to make a point rather than words
- ✓ Use a quote or a picture to emphasise a point
  If short on time, skip slides without the audience knowing. You do this by inserting the new slide number and pressing enter. Prior to the presentation you must take a note of the sections of your PowerPoint presentation (in slide view). Place a "post it" with these details on the side

of your screen. If you need to skip to the next section by passing slides, you will know where the next section starts, as that will be on the post it. For example if the next section starts at slide 50, you put in 50 on the keyboard and press return and the presentation goes straight to slide 50.

✓ If you want the audience to just look at you for a moment, you can press:

✓ "B" key - Blank the screen

✓ "W" key - White the screen

✓ Have a remote mouse so that you can change slides from any part of the room.

Do's and don'ts

✓ Always make the slides look slick and have a clear purpose

✓ Always use colour to put your message across

✓ Always use slides that represent your brand, what you represent.

✓ Always check spellings

✓ Always have a rehearsal on a big screen

✓ Always carry a backup presentation

✓ Always date your presentation and personalise it

✓ Never use other people's slides without customising them for yourself

✓ Never read the slides

✓ Never use more than 5 bullet points and 5 words per bullet point per slide

✓ Never use flashy custom animation – it will distract from your purpose

✓ Never use a slide until you have asked yourself the purpose it is performing

✓ Never use too many pictures on one slide

W Mitchell one of the very best speakers in the USA says "Average speakers, if they do use PowerPoint, should have no more than 10 slides, use them for no more than 20 minutes and never have smaller font than 30"

This is known as the 10, 20, 30 rule

Section 3

Tip Top Tips

1 *Decide what you want to achieve before you start. Start with the end in mind.*

2 *Visual aids are there to show people how the point of the presentation will benefit them. Not as a script for the presenter.*

3 *PowerPoint is a fantastic visual aid used properly. It can be a disaster used unprofessionally.*

4 *Demonstrate whenever you can.*

5 *Team presentations are beneficial as long as everyone knows what their roles are.*

My Notes

My Notes

_____

_____

_____

_____

_____

_____

_____

_____

_____

_____

_____

_____

_____

_____

_____

_____

_____

_____

SECTION 4

Energy

> *Energy is contagious.*
> *You catch positive energy and*
> *you catch negative energy*
>
> *Dr Wayne Dyer*

Remember energy is contagious. So you need to lead the energy level – you are the leader.

During the presentation you must be thinking not just about the delivery of your content, but the energy of the audience.

By managing your energy and selecting the right balance of content, you can make a substantial difference to the energy levels in the room and therefore the enjoyment of the audience. Vary the energy levels.

Whilst you should be emitting positive energy throughout the presentation you do need to vary your energy. It is no good starting high and getting ever higher until you come across as manic. You need a positive start, building in pace and energy and then coming back down slightly, perhaps to emphasise a particularly complex or important point

If you sense the room energy is low (clues include lots of bowed heads, sleepy eyes, and people folding arms or leaning on their elbows), there are lots of things you can do. If the room is getting hot, have a door or windows opened or have the air conditioning adjusted. Then change the pace of the presentation by opening up for a role play, an activity or questions.

A very effective strategy, if appropriate, is to give the audience a two minute break. However, ensure they do get up and stretch their legs. I might ask the audience to discuss something with their colleague next to them or to find someone else in the room to discuss it with. This creates interaction but more importantly re-adjusts the energy.

NOTE - It can be very difficult for people who are used to moving about all day to be sitting at a lecture or a talk or a training course for a longer than normal period.

If you are struggling to increase your own energy, here are some of the tips professionals use:

1 Remind yourself that you are there for the audience's benefit.
2 It's your responsibility to help them, with your knowledge
3 You can rest later - give 100% now
4 Pattern interrupt (see below)

Do something for effect to change the thinking of the audience. One of the most effective things I have seen done, but it is risky, is suddenly saying to the audience "can you smell anything?" – suggesting the presenter could smell smoke.

The whole audience switched on their reptilian part of the brain, which alerts us to danger. Having satisfied themselves there was no danger people were back in the present, listening.

Be careful if you use something like this, as people wouldn't like to think you had tricked them.

> *"It is not necessary to change*
> *- survival is not mandatory"*
>
> *W Edwards Deming*

How to handle the graveyard session

The graveyard session, as it is called is the session after lunch when our circadian rhythms can be at their lowest.

Circadian rhythms occur about every 90 minutes giving us a high or a low alternatively. In the early morning they are at their lowest and in fact our bodies slow down more than any time at between 2.00am and 3.00am and also in the afternoon slots of 2.00pm – 3.00pm. Additionally, after lunch the body is digesting food, which always takes energy, and can be a difficult time for attention spans.

If you have a choice, this might not be the best time to present. If you have to present at this time, you will have to have even more energy and interest to keep your audience with you. You might prefer to negotiate the timings with the organiser to avoid this session.

The mediocre teacher tells.
The good teacher explains.
The superior teacher demonstrates.
The great teacher inspires."

William Arthur Ward - Author, Editor and Pastor

Questions

> *"The quality of the questions you ask, determines the quality of the answers you get"*
>
> *Peter Thomson*

It is important with any presentation to be prepared for questions and manage them effectively.

At the start of your presentation, in the introduction, tell the audience when you will take questions. That might be at any time, at the start or the end of sessions or at certain breaks in the presentation.

When the time comes state clearly "I will now take questions" – this prompts the audience to ask questions - rather than asking the closed question "Are there any questions?"

Allow time in your planning for questions and answers (Q+A) within your allotted slot.

Some speakers like to have a Q+A before their summary or close so that they can still end on a high. If you have summarised and then there are questions it can lead to an ending which does not emphasise the positives and leaves the audience feeling low. I recommend taking questions and then summarising with your key points.

If you have a concern about questions, you need to practise answers to likely or difficult questions. If you know your subject you will be able to brainstorm all the likely questions from the presentation. Write these down and then write out the answers and practice them until they become natural. If you don't know your subject ask yourself "Should I be presenting this subject?"

If you are addressing questions to the audience you can ask questions in certain ways.

An <u>open question</u> usually starts with" What, How, Tell me what are your thoughts on?... Could you explain?

Make sure these questions are used selectively and appropriately.

Be careful with questions that begin with Why? Why suggests you are challenging the other person and almost always puts them on the back foot. Reframe the question in a slightly better way.

A <u>closed question</u> usually only elicits a "yes" or "no" answer and calls for no further comment.

REMEMBER HIGH QUALITY QUESTIONS ARE BEST PREPARED IN ADVANCE – these are ones that lead the audience in a certain direction. The direction in which you wish them to go.

"Yes tag" questions that are aimed at getting the audience to agree with the statement you have just made. They can be used to build rapport.

For example

"It's a great day out there today! Isn't it?

"That was a very average lunch! Wasn't it?

"We will all be ready for our coffee break
– won't we?

In these cases the audience will answer "Yes" with their voice or at very least in their mind and you will see them nodding.

"No tag" questions. Naturally people would rather answer no to a question if they are not sure. This is a natural defensive action. Therefore no tag questions can be used like this to get agreement.

"Is there anything else you need to know before we move on?"

"Is there anything else you need to know before we complete the paper work?

It may be used by sales people as a trial close or to find out if there is anything else the client needs to know.

Listening Skills

> "Most people need a good listening
> to, instead of a good talking to"
>
> *Anon*

Very few people are good at listening. It's strange really that we listen to our mother's heartbeat whilst we are in the womb and then it is taken for granted for the rest of our lives that we are good listeners. The truth is that not many people listen properly.

The most effective listening is whole body listening which is with your ears, your eyes and all your senses.

Listening to exactly what the person is really saying; or what the person isn't saying.

As presenters we have to listen to our client, the person who is employing us, to the audience and to the individuals within the audience.

Top tips, to listen properly

1. Maintain upright positive body language;
   be ready to make notes when required and show a genuine interest in what the other person is saying.
2. Repeat back for clarity and summarise at intervals to check understanding.
3. Remember that we speak at up to 200 words a minute and can think and listen at over 800 words a minute. That helps us focus our minds on concentrating on the other person.

Some fun you can have with people to test their listening skills -

Ask-

1. How many animals of each species did Moses take into the ark?
2. What is the correct English - Nine and five is thirteen or nine and five are thirteen
3. How is your maths? You are the driver of a bus; there are 37 people on the bus. At Trafalgar Sq. 8 people get on, 5 get off. At Oxford Circus, 10 get off and 4 get on. OK so far. What's the name of the bus driver?

As you know Moses didn't have an Ark, it was Noah. Nine and five are 14 and YOU are the driver of the bus. See how many people REALLY listen.

The learning point here is that people anticipate what you are going to say next, rather than listening to what you actually say. Their mind opens a window, rather like the filing system on your computer, and then assumes what is going to be said. This is called preconditioning in psychology; we have all been preconditioned when we were in altered states of consciousness by things our parents might have said to us. For example, if you don't eat your carrots you won't be able to see in the dark.

Equipment

If presenting regularly, you need to think about having your own equipment, as hotel or conference centre equipment will often let you down.

You should arrive early and have arranged to meet the room manager to check that the equipment works. This sometimes gives you the opportunity to change the seating from formal to informal, theatre style to oval, which is less formal. Discuss the tea and coffee breaks and where you want them. Rather than where they want them. I would encourage you to have refreshments outside the main room so you don't get disturbed when they arrive. This also encourages the audience to have a change of scenery, which in turn changes the energy levels.

This is some of the equipment I might take to a presentation.

> Computer projector (back up one if necessary)
> Speakers
> Power leads
> Extension leads
> Remote mouse
> DVD – or built in one in my computer
> Video clips
> Flip charts or flip charts paper.
> Flip chart pens
> Mini flip chart - A4 / A3 pad turned landscape
> Client pitch books
> Audience work books
> Post it notes

Language

Use language that everyone can understand. Winston Churchill one of the greatest orators, is quoted as saying "use plain English".

Jargon. Be very careful with jargon. People in different industries use all sorts of jargon and expect others to understand. By all means use jargon if you know your audience will understand. However make absolutely certain they do understand the jargon by checking their understanding. People will often say they do when they don't, to avoid being embarrassed. You are the communicator and it is your responsibility to make sure that the audience understands.

I was speaking recently to a group of bankers and using the phrase "Basis points". A basis point is one hundredth of one percent which is used by finance people but rarely understood outside their industry. I had assumed that all bankers would know the meaning of this. However on seeing some slight frowning in the audience (it is vital to watch the body language) I found that some of the group had not heard of this phrase. I was able to explain it and have everybody back on my side.

Slang – Be careful with slang, It usually doesn't cross cultures and certainly will take some authority away from you, unless it is used for a specific purpose.

One of the best communicators in America is Nido Quibein. In his book, "How to be a Great

Communicator", he gives an example of how the word "slug" can be used in different contexts.

1 You drink a slug of orange juice in the morning before leaving for work.
2 You see in a movie that doctors are removing a .22 calibre slug from the shoulder of a robbery victim.
3 As you step outside your front door you step on a slug that has crawled across the path.
4 When you get to work your colleague tells you he has been slugging it out, working on his book all night.

When I was studying at the US National Speakers Conference at Marco Island University in Florida, I was having dinner with a speaker from Dallas, Tim Durkin, and he was explaining something to me. I said "OK the penny has now dropped". He had no idea what I was talking about. In the UK this means we now realise what is happening. The phrase came from vending machines which used pennies and wouldn't work until the penny had dropped into the operating slot.

"Check your slang"

Swearing. Use of obscenities has no place in presenting. It almost always devalues what the person is saying and devalues them in the eyes of the audience. I have known people use it to try and build rapport but in virtually every case it fails and backfires on the presenter.

Gender
Use both male and female at all times and you cannot upset anyone.

Body language

How you look is very important. Showing confident body language will help you gain credibility with your audience.

Posture –
> An alert erect posture signifies interest and involvement.

> A slouching posture says "I am not really interested in exchanging ideas with you".

> A stiff rigid posture says "I don't feel fully comfortable in your presence".

An upright posture gives you confidence and conveys a confident authority to your audience.

Eye contact / gaze control – make eye contact around the room. However make sure you are looking out to the back of the room and the sides.

It will come naturally once your confidence builds. Get a friend or a coach to observe and check.

Do not hold eye contact with some one for too long unless they are asking you a question. Then repeat the question for the benefit of the whole audience. This enables you to answer the question for the individual and the audience. It also avoids you talking to just the one person and looking like you are leaving the whole group out.

Openness
Audiences don't warm to, listen to or believe presenters who use closed body language, so make your gestures warm and open. If you are asked a difficult question, don't bluff – any signs of lying or deception will be apparent in your body language. Watch politicians and model the best.

Audience body language
Take note of the body language of the audience and respond to it. This will enable you to keep their energy positive and their learning level high. If, for example, more than 10% of people have their arms crossed, maybe its time for a re-energising exercise or a coffee break. But be careful not to misread individual gestures; some people can look sceptical when they are evaluating what the presenter has just said.

There will inevitably be a variety of personalities in the audience with different issues going on in their heads. Try not to pick on an individual who appears by his/her body language to be disinterested. They may have just had a terrible row with their partner and have other things on their mind. Make sure their issue doesn't affect you.

Finally
If you are in a small group, you may decide to sit down from time-to-time, for effect and to gain rapport. Don't sit for very long as you will need to keep your status and control. Avoid using lecterns unless it is a very formal presentation with lots of technical content. If you do have to use a lectern, make sure you move away from it to make key points. If you are using PowerPoint, keep it fast and energetic.

If you are not sure why a slide is on the screen your body language will give you away. Try to examine the point of each slide you use and, if it is not clear, dispense with the slide.

Voice control

A voice coach works with me and gives me voice control exercises. How you use your voice is important. Both Margaret Thatcher and George Bush employed a voice coach to help them lower their voice an octave. Their credibility ratings went up enormously after they had learned this technique.

We give strength and confidence to the audience when we speak with a low pitched, well modulated voice. When the voice rises to a high pitch; we sense excitement, panic and lack of control.

We should use the lower end of our voice range when we want to communicate calmness, confidence and competence.

Through our voice quality we can convey feelings, moods and attitudes. These are sometimes called paralanguage and can be created by speed intonation, volume and pace.

Volume and pace should be carefully controlled. They can be used together to create powerful effects. You can let your voice rise to a crescendo or drop to a whisper depending on the effect you want to create.

You should make sure every member of the audience can hear you, which may mean wearing a microphone.

Section 4
Tip Top Tips

1 *Energise yourself before the presentation and then transmit your presentation to the delegates.*

2 *Spot energy lows from the body language. Handle them in a professional way which allows the audience members to recover their energy.*

3 *Take questions, anticipate them and listen carefully.*

4 *Have the best equipment available to keep the audience interested.*

5 *Give out great body language, voice skills and language skills. Practice, practice and practice again.*

My Notes

My Notes

SECTION 5

Extroverts and Introverts

"Which type of person are you? There are both types in each audience"

In general -

Extroverts like to gain energy from talking to others, getting on and doing things and learning by practice.

Introverts like to gain energy from within and learn by reading, thinking and watching (mental practice). They direct energy towards their inner world of experience and ideas.

So what does this mean for presenters and audiences?

Extrovert presenters –

- ✓ Need to be careful not to talk too much.
- ✓ They have strength in engaging (with other extroverts) in the audience.
- ✓ May rush – need to slow down, watch the audience for clues (are they interested or are they asleep?)

✓ Do not mind being interrupted.

✓ They tend to speak first and reflect later, so you might need to be careful in answering questions.

✓ Are good at developing ideas through discussion, so there could be other opportunities that come up at the questioning stage.

✓ Are mostly interested in activities and how other people achieve things.

Introvert presenters -

✓ Need to be careful to promote external visible energy within the presentation.

✓ Will probably be good at handling questions and listening, provided they do not take too long to go within themselves for the answers.

✓ Have trouble remembering names and faces.

✓ May prefer to present alone, "This is my project".

✓ Don't like being interrupted.

✓ Can have trouble communicating, because it is all in their head.

✓ Prefer to communicate in writing (the dreaded email communicator) so the slides might be busy. (See section under PowerPoint for best practice).

✓ Are often interested in facts and ideas. The presentation could be dry.

Extrovert audiences – like variety and action. Get impatient with slow paced presentations. Will want to ask questions and may interrupt.

Extroverts may think Introverts are withholding information when they are processing information internally.

Introvert audiences - like quieter presentations, for concentration, so they can understand and relate points back to themselves. They will take longer to ask questions, as they will want to think first.

Introverts may think that Extroverts are changing their minds when they are actually processing a decision verbally.

Summary

There are opportunities to spot the types and work with them according to the style of the presenter or the presentation. The art is to recognise, understand and appreciate the different styles.

Mental Rehearsal

Before you are going to give or make an important presentation, imagine you are on the podium, on the stage or at the company giving the talk, smoothly, clearly and effectively. Imagine what you will say, how you will say it, and what gestures you will use.

Imagine yourself feeling confident and energised. AND imagine the standing ovation at the end – or that successful feeling from a job well done.

You can practice mental rehearsal for sensitive conversations, sales presentations or meetings with Boards of Directors.

I always mentally rehearse the night before just as I am falling asleep, in that alpha state of consciousness, and sometimes I get an extra idea which makes a real difference.

Mindmapping

Mindmapping is a very powerful tool in presenting. It can be used to enhance your professionalism in many ways.

If you have to give a near spontaneous presentation with only a few minutes to prepare. Drawing a mindmap will help your brain release all of your thoughts on to paper, in a sequence which will help you present, clearly and concisely.

I know a number of people who mindmap before a presentation whether it be to the Chief Executive of a company, a board or a credit committee.

Mindmapping before a presentation, or even an exam, helps you to recall information in a situation where you might be anxious or your mind goes blank.

How to mindmap

All you need to begin Mindmapping is the topic, a few coloured pens, and a large sheet of plain paper.

These are the rules that make a mind map work best, although I would encourage you to try it your own way.

1.   Use the paper, landscape preferably, with no lines. Begin your mind map with a word, symbol or a picture (representing your topic) at the centre of your page. Starting at the centre opens your mind to a full

360 degrees of association. Pictures and symbols are much easier to remember than words and enhance your ability to think creatively about your subject.

2. Write down key words. Key words are the information-rich "nuggets" of recall and creative association.

3. Connect the key words with lines radiating from your central image.

4. By linking words with lines ("branches"), you'll show clearly how one key word relates to another.

5. Print your key words. Printing is easier to read and remember than writing.

6. Print one key word per line. By doing this, you free yourself to discover the maximum number of creative associations for each key word. The discipline of one word per line also trains you to focus on the most appropriate key word, enhancing the precision of your thought and minimizing clutter.

7. Print your key words on the lines and make the length of the word the same as the line it is on. This maximizes clarity of association and encourages economy of space.

8. Use colours, pictures, codes and jargon for greater association and emphasis.

9. Highlight important points and illustrate relationships between different branches of your mind map. You might, for instance, prioritise your main points through colour coding, highlighting in yellow the most important points, using blue for secondary points, and so forth. Pictures and images, preferably in vivid colour, should be used wherever possible; they stimulate your creative association and greatly enhance your memory.

Telephone Presentations

We mentioned pitch books and tender documents which sometimes might be sent by mail, which means you don't get the chance to present them. This is never to be recommended but it does happen sometimes.

It is important to mention presentations by telephone. It's extraordinary that many people don't put the same amount of effort into a telephone presentation as they might do to a face to face one.

However, these can be just as important and may be your only chance. In these circumstances you cannot see the body language. You are now relying on voice tonality, energy and the language we use. You cannot see the client and it is more difficult to check for understanding.

Therefore, proper preparation should take place with objectives, outcome and agenda at the front of your mind. Perhaps with a mindmap, cue cards or a mini flip chart.

I even sometimes put my verbal presentation on a flip chart I have in my office. It makes me concentrate on the importance of the presentation. I can see it clearly from a distance and stand up whilst talking, which makes my voice sound stronger and conveys authority.

Electronic Presentations

Video link

Video link presentations can be difficult as it is not always easy to give and see the body language clearly. Actors have been trained to exaggerate gestures and features so this can be picked up by the audiences. You may have to do this to make points clearer for the receiver. Practice and feedback will increase your effectiveness.

If you have to present by video conferencing make sure you are sharp, prepared and have practised.

Email

If you are emailing a presentation to a client make sure it is in a professional format. One of the simpler formats is in PDF format and it also maintains consistency.

If you are in the legal profession or dealing with litigious issues make sure you email documents in a form in which they cannot be altered.

Content v Performance

> *"Great presentation skills are the one laser fix to enhance your results"*
>
> *Nido Quibane*

There should be a balance between content and performance. The more interesting you can make the presentation, the more people will enjoy it and the more they will learn.

Because different people have different learning styles a balance will always be needed. However, by varying your performance between visual, auditory and experiential, the learning experience will be fast tracked into more knowledge in a shorter time for more people.

Visual -

      Slides

      Flip chart

      Physical examples

      Video clips

Auditory / Verbal -

      Lecturing

      Talking

Experiential -

Discuss this amongst yourselves

Come up with 5 unique selling points for your product

Use a case study

Micro simulation

Simulation

Exercise

Closing

Closing is about making sure that you have achieved your goal. It is often just about asking the audience / customer / client for the piece of business or to take action towards the goal.

The questions to ask yourself when closing your presentations are:

✓ Have I covered everything?

✓ If I haven't, does it matter?

✓ What was my goal?

> Have I achieved it?

> If I haven't - can I do anything about it now or later?

✓ Have I reminded the audience about what I have told them?

✓ Do I have a further goal at the end to interest the client in other products / issues?

✓ Are there action points to be agreed? If so can we agree those jointly?

If it is to close a piece of business, say

> *"I look forward to working with you in the future".*

Or

> *"It would be great to do this piece of business with you".*

If it is to enhance the learning:-

> Set up a mastermind group, mastermind groups (small focused group of like minded people determined to help each other succeed).

> Set up buddy groups (two or three people aimed at challenging and assisting each other).

Summary

This is as important as the start. It should always be after the questions and answers session. It should summarise what has been said in three points and it should be motivational for the audience to take action.

Remember the power of threes. Threes have rhythm, credibility and sound right.

If you summarise before the question and answer session you might be remembered for the quality of that session rather than your real message. So make sure your summary comes afterwards.

Example finish

"Ladies and Gentlemen thank you for listening to me. I want to remind you that presentation skills are some of the most important skills that you can develop.

You may be changing people's lives by what you tell them; how you present; and the message you send them away with.

"My name is Derek Arden; I wish you every success with your presentations, your business careers and with everything you do. Have a great day".

Section 5

Tip Top Tips

1 *Mindmap your presentations before you start to write them.*

2 *Mentally rehearse the presentation several times.*

3 *There should be a balance between content and performance. The presentation needs to be made interesting and exciting to get the message across to your audience.*

4 *Summarise and tell the audience what you told them and what they might do next.*

5 *When you close, check if you have reached your goal.*

My Notes

SECTION 6

Frequently asked questions

What do I do if the equipment fails in the middle of my session?

1 - You should always have a contingency plan for failure of equipment. A well prepared presenter should be able to present well without any equipment.

This means you do have to have back up copies of things that need to be visually shown.

I was doing a presentation for Henley Management College at the Barclays University in Manchester when there was a fire alarm, a real one. Immediately the Director from Henley asked me if I would take the delegates over to a Starbucks coffee restaurant and continue by having a question and answer session over there. She then said, "Derek, at the same time you can show everybody how good a negotiator you are by getting a discount on all the coffees".

I don't know what I was more concerned about, the informal style of the new presentation, regular Starbucks customers listening in, or having to negotiate a discount in a place which I wasn't sure gave discounts. I got the discount and the session in Starbucks went really well.

2 - If something goes wrong with your computer, remember it has happened to most presenters.

Secondly, don't hide the fact and, depending how familiar you are with your computer; logically go through what the issues might be.

Here are some of the more common faults

1. Power lead not connected properly and battery flat.
2. PowerPoint has jumped to last slide because you accidentally pressed the end slide.
3. Computer overloaded and you have to reboot.

Share with the audience what has happened and put into place your contingency plan.

How can I animate my presentation? I am nervous about anything complicated.

Be careful with animation.

Ask yourself why you want to animate the presentation.

✓ Is it to make it more interesting for you?
✓ Is it to make the presentation more interesting for the audience?
✓ Is it because you have just learnt how to use animation and you want to show off?
✓ What is the effect of what I am going to do on the audience?
✓ Does it make my point clearer?
✓ Does it confuse the issue?

Often it can confuse the point and the audience are more interested in working out from which direction the next animation is coming.

Sit back and re-evaluate what you are trying to achieve. If it works, use it. Be honest with yourself

What if there is a fire alarm and the building is evacuated? How do I get restarted?

Keep your cool. The most important issue is the safety of the audience. Don't joke that it is probably a false alarm. Ask if there is anybody in the audience who knows whether there was going to be a test today. (You should have checked this already). If not, take safety action. You can always pick up from where you left off.

How do I handle interruptions? How do I deal with delegates who seem to want to monopolise the questions?

Make sure that you don't put them down in the minds of the rest of the audience. If you do, there is a big danger that the rest of the audience will side with the other person.

The best way to handle this is to respect the other person's opinion and say to them that you will take that point off line at the break. Make sure that you do so.

How do I answer difficult questions?

As you are an expert by being the speaker, you need to anticipate difficult questions. We cannot always answer every question we are given. At that stage we have choices -

Answer with your own opinion if you are reasonably sure of the answer.

Answer saying that "I will find out". However make sure that you qualify the question, and ensure that you understand what the real question is that the person is asking. Sometimes people ask difficult questions just to test us when they know the answer themselves.

What do I do when someone is late?

This depends on the circumstances. If most people are there then I believe you should start on time. If you don't, you are penalising the people who arrived on time. If there has been a problem on the motorway and there are a number of people phoning in and apologising, then you could decide to start informally and formally start when everybody has arrived.

What do I do if people start talking when I am speaking?

You need to ask yourself why they are talking.

Are they talking because they do not understand a point? If so it may be the other audience members do not understand the point either. Further clarification could be needed.

Are they talking because they are being rude? If so, just moving over and showing by your body language that you understand what they are doing may stop it.

You could stop and give the group a break and find out what the issue is and clarify it.

Are they talking because the energy levels are low and they want to have a break themselves? Have a look at everybody else and have a short sharp break.

"Remember less is often more"

60 second reminders

What is the objective of the presentation?
What is the outcome you want?
What might your agenda look like?

Remember WIIFM (What's in it for me) – Reverse it for "What's in it for the audience?"
Write out - mind map – 5 x 3 cards or bigger
Simple visual aids – 10 / 20 / 30 rule

Summarise
Tell them - tell them - tell them
Questions and answers

Be Enthusiastic - Be Fantastic

Warning

No responsibility for lack of success can be taken if you under-prepare

---

If you think you are beaten, you are
If you think you dare not, you won't
If you like to win, but you think you can't
It is almost certain that you won't

If you think you will lose, you're lost
For out of the world we find,
Success begins with will
It's all in the state of mind

If you think you are outclassed, you are
You have got to think high to rise,
You have got to be sure of yourself before
You can ever win a prize

Life's battles don't always go
To the strongest or faster man
But sooner or later the man who wins
Is the man WHO THINKS HE CAN

From Think and Grow Rich by Napoleon Hill 1937

Check list

What are my objectives for this presentation?

What is the outcome I want for the audience?

What is my most effective agenda?

On a scale of 0 -----10

Where am I on this presentation?

How close can I get to 10?

How close should I get to 10?

How important is it?

Do I need some help?

Do I need a template?

Do I need to get others up to speed?

Aide memoire

FAST TRACK REMINDERS

✓ Preparation – research.

✓ Build rapport and empathy.
- Tell them what you are going to tell them
- Tell them
- Tell them what you have told them

✓ 30 second intro – 30 second close.

✓ Choose your visuals carefully.

✓ Positive language.

✓ Positive body language

✓ Project your voice with confidence.

✓ Summarise, thank and close.

✓ Ask for a further commitment.

10 most feared things

From a well reported New York Times survey

Amazingly in this order

Public speaking

Death

Heights

Insects

Financial Problems

Deep Water

Sickness

Flying

Loneliness

Dogs

Questions to ask your client or sponsor

How many people will be at the conference?

What would you like me to achieve in the time available?

Who are the important people in the audience?

What previous speakers have you had?

How long have I got?

Will anybody introduce me?

>   Who will it be?

>   Would they like me to send them an introduction?

Is there time for questions?

May I have the questions before I close?

How else can I help you?

Recommended reading

Life is a Series of Presentations - Tony Jeary

The Secrets of Communication - Peter Thomson

The Ultimate Book of Mind Mapping - Tony Buzan

Speed Reading - Tony Buzan

How to be a Great Communicator - Nido Quibein

7 Habits of Highly Effective People - Steven Covey

Presenting Magically - Tad James and David Shephard

Presentation Skills for Dummies - Malcolm Kushner

The Magic of Thinking Big - Dr David Schwartz

Influence Science and Practice - Robert Cialdini

Success Intelligence - Robert Holden

Can you Spot the Gorilla - Richard Wiseman

Quirkology - Richard Wiseman

The Power of the Sub-Conscious Mind - Dr Joseph Murphy

Blink - Macolm Gladwell

Walk Tall - Lesley Everett

How to be Brilliant - Michael Heppell

Change your Life in 7 days - Paul McKenna

The Confidence Factor - Paul McKenna

Unlimited Power - Anthony Robbins

PowerPoint skills - Marylyn Schneider

The Ultimate Book on Body Language - Allan and Barbara Pease

How to Win Friends and Influence People - Dale Carnegie

Mans Search for Meaning – Viktor Frankel

Luck Factor - Richard Wiseman

Unlimited Success – Napoleon Hill

The Mind Gym – The mind gym

Super Coach – Graham Alexander, Ben Renshaw

Recommended Audio Resources

The Achievers Edge - Nightingale Conant

Live with Passion - Tony Robbins

How to Communicate like a Pro – Nido Quibein

The Ultimate audio programme on body language –
Allan and Barbara Pease

Luck – Denis Waitley

Glossary

Alpha state of consciousness - The relaxed state of mind, when you are just falling asleep, waking up or doing something unrelated.

Anchoring - A process whereby a stimulus or representation gets connected to a response. Anchors can be set up intentionally but are likely to have occurred naturally. They can be helpful or unhelpful.

Automatic compliance - The pre-programmed response to a verbal trigger. e.g. Yes tag or No tag questions.

Chunking - Moving up and down from detail to the bigger picture.

Circadian rhythms - Energy rhythms, which we all have. Having a high point in our energy and a low point 90 minutes later.

Commitment and consistency principle - The tendency of people not to want to change the ways of doing something once they have taken steps to start and go in a particular direction.

Double bind – Giving a person a choice, where the objective is for them to agree to one or the other. Which one you don't mind eg. Would you like to go to bed at 10pm or 10.30pm or would you like to finish at 5.00pm or 4.45pm?

Future pacing - Focusing the mind of the audience on the pleasant outcome of a requested action.

Hierarchy of needs - From Abraham Maslow who wrote about the 5 stages that dictate our basic desires. Food and sex, shelter and safety, belonging and social contact, esteem and status, self fulfilment.

Host introduction - The opportunity for somebody else to acquaint the audience with the presenter's background, highlight the content of the presentation, and comment on the importance of the material to the audience. A strong host will enhance the presenter's credibility and open the audience's minds to the ideas being conveyed.

Law of requisite variety - In any system of machines or human beings, the element or person with the widest range of options will become the controlling factor in that system.

Leading - Generating a new response in the other person.

Liking principle - Our tendency to be receptive to messages from people who like us or are like us.

Mental state - The frame of mind the person is in that may affect his or her receptivity to a message or the ability to deliver a presentation effectively.

Micro-simulation - a case study / role play that is done in a very short period of time and often on an ad-hoc or spontaneous basis.

Macro-simulation - a case study / role play where the presenter (s) plays one role and the whole audience plays (say) the client. The lead presenter switches between client and coach by assuming one role when sitting and one role when standing.

Mindmapping - Creative way to write your presentation in landscape with links, lines, keywords, pictures which stimulate creativity and memory retention.

Mind set – When a person is in a fixed way of thinking.

Mirroring - Subtle copying of another person's posture, gestures, body language, tone of voice and language in order to facilitate rapport.

Muscle memory - Behaviour so ingrained by repetition that it has become almost automatic.

Nested loops - A technique that exploits the audience's natural desire for completion. This maintains their attention by interrupting a story and then moving onto other things only to return to the original story later.

Neuro linguistic Programming (NLP) - The study and use of language as it impacts the brain and therefore our behaviour. A study of excellence that models how the highest achievers structure their experience.

Pacing - What practitioners in NLP call the process of matching behaviours and beliefs of the audience.

Parking - Putting issues and questions into an area to deal with at the end.

Pattern interrupt - Breaking undesirable patterns of behaviour or thinking, by introducing an abrupt change.

Peer trust transference - The employment of social proof to earn the confidence of the audience through the use of words or other reinforcement from an audience or peers.

Planned spontaneity - Prior preparation that enables you to respond to an audience when something unforeseen goes wrong.

Political mapping - Assessing the importance of various people in a meeting / presentation to determine the impact they may have on your desired outcomes.

Presentation world - All the presentation opportunities in your life, both professional and personal.

Rapport - The sense of connection that puts you on the same wavelength as the other person or group.

Reciprocation principle - The deep, usually unconscious, sense that we have an obligation to repay a debt, favour or concession.

Relearning - Things that we know but we don't put into practice.

Scarcity principle - The inclination to desire things we believe are in short supply, including information.

Sensory acuity - The employment of our senses, sight, hearing, feeling, smell and taste to a lesser degree, in order to understand the audience and the environment in which a presentation is being made. It is also the learning how to make more accurate sense of the information we receive from the world.

Sensory modalities - The way we receive information, usually with a preference for visual, auditory or kinaesthetic modes.

Social proof principle - The sense that we have more confidence in a given course of action because other people have done it or acted in that way. Examples include testimonials, endorsements and reference letters.

Stages of learning - The four steps in our mastery of a skill from unconscious incompetence, to conscious incompetence, conscious competence to unconscious competence (automatic performance)

Subconscious desires - The eight needs for every audience member to belong, to be respected, to be liked, to be safe, to succeed, to find romance, to be inspired and enthused.

Surveying for content - Asking beforehand in a survey where members of the audience stand on issues that will come up and determining how they might best be presented.

WOW points - Things we are immediately going to take action on.

Resources

To help you in your series of life presentations, you and your company, Derek Arden International's fast track resources are at your service.

Professional Conference Speaking

Facilitation – Strategic Awaydays

Chairing and Hosting

Masterclasses – Negotiating, Influencing and

Presenting

Train the trainers

Training and self development materials

Business consulting

Profitability consulting

Negotiation advice

Handling tough people

Mentoring and coaching

Presentation writing

Return on investment calculations

Assessments and solutions

Non executive adviser

Banking solutions

Negotiation with third party clients

For articles, downloads, newsletters, advice
www.derekarden.co.uk
www.negotiating-succcess.com
www.derekarden.blogspot.com

For free email newsletter - email derek@derekarden.co.uk

How to contact the team at Derek Arden Fast Track resources.

We are located in Guildford, Surrey close to London and both London Heathrow and London Gatwick airports. We have associates in Leicester, Edinburgh, Perth, Western Australia, Dubai, United States, Canada and New Zealand

Telephone numbers
00 44 (0) 1483 505854
00 44 (0) 1483 532880 Fax
Website www.derekarden.co.uk

Mailing and shipping address
PO Box 974
Guildford, Surrey, GU19BR
United Kingdom
By email – action@derekarden.co.uk

Final thoughts

People think in pictures and have to be associated with the issues themselves to generate strong emotional responses. This is why stories are so effective in backing up your presentations.

Stories are all around you so there is no need to use other peoples. Look for your own stories as you raise your sensory acuity and start thinking about the next presentation.

It's funny how things just have a knack of coming to us when we know what we are looking for. As Louis Pasteur said after he invented penicillin:

"Chance favours the prepared mind"

Afterword

I am passionate about helping others help themselves. This is with knowledge, education and inspiration.

As it says in many great teachings since the great Greek philosophers.

"You can give a person a fish OR you can teach a person to fish".

PASS THIS BOOK OR JUST SOME OF THE SUITABLE PAGES ON TO OTHERS. ENCOURAGE, ASSIST AND HELP THEM IMPROVE.

Derek Arden

PO Box 974
Guildford,
Surrey,
United Kingdom

Our presentations are always work in progress

Quick order form

Fax orders – 00 44 1483 532880. Send this form

Telephone orders – Tiptree House Publishing 00 44 1483 505854

Email orders – action@derekarden.co.uk

Cheques orders – Derek Arden International Ltd
Tiptree House publishing
POBox 974
Guildford, Surrey, GU19BR United Kingdom

*Please send the following books, CD's reports. I understand that
I may return any of them for a full refund – for any reason,
no questions asked.*

....

....

....

Please send me FREE information on

- ☐ **Other books**
- ☐ **Speaking / seminars**
- ☐ **Consulting**
- ☐ **Mentoring and coaching**
- ☐ **Profitability**

Name ....

Address ....

....

City ....

Telephone ....

Email address ....

Shipping by air
Please add £2 for 1st book or CD and £1 for each additional product